MEMORY MAKERS

MEMORY MAKERS

50 MOMENTS YOUR KIDS WILL NEVER FORGET

DOUG FIELDS & DUFFY ROBBINS

Youth Specialties

ZondervanPublishingHouse
Grand Rapids, Michigan
A Division of HarperCollinsPublishers

To our friends on the Youth Specialties National Resource Seminar Team: Ridge Burns, Chap Clark, Ray Johnston, Tic Long, Marv Penner, Laurie Polich, and Mike Yaconelli. It seems that whenever we put our heads together to create memories for teenagers, we create memories for ourselves as well.

TABLE OF CONTENTS

INDEX

INTRODUCTION

This book is not about mere nostalgia—or sentimentalism, or living in a time warp, or trying to live in the past. This book is about making memories for your students today so your youth group will be different tomorrow.

Frankly, we think memories are underrated. It's easy to think about memories in the past tense: *spilt milk, water over the dam, those were the days.* We forget about the present power of memory—we forget that memory is a paintbrush that brings vivid color to special moments, old songs, favorite stories, incredible experiences, painful lessons, and hard times. Memories are the milestones by which we mark our journeys with God.

Yet some gauge the health of a youth group by the number of Bible posters and Christian banners on the youth room walls. If you really want to get in touch with the spiritual history of a group, though, look for photos of kids. That's where the real stories of faith are told—kids rafting together, kids becalmed at all-night truck stops because the bus broke down, kids posing in front of a two-room home they made for a third-world family, their arms around each other's shoulders, realizing the difference they actually made in others' lives. Such snapshots capture the grace and goodness of God.

Face it—few of us (teenager, child, *or* adult)

remember sermons and Bible studies, workshops and classes—or even, for that matter, skits and games. We're much more likely to remember random moments—episodes during which we are surprised by the unexpected, touched by a sense of genuine community, consumed by an experience so real that it replays itself often in our minds. "We have heard," wrote St. John in his first letter, "we have seen with our eyes...we have looked at and our hands have touched...this we proclaim." Memories are the threads with which God weaves genuine faith.

Go into all the world—and make memories

In his second letter to Timothy, St. Paul wrote words that he sensed would be his last to his young disciple. No doubt he chose them carefully. Yet you can't help notice when you read the apostle's words that his charge to his pastoral protégé Timothy was not so much a sermon, lesson, or classroom lecture as it was a plea that Timothy draw from a rich portfolio of memories. "You," Paul wrote to him, "know all about my teaching, my way of life, my purpose, faith, patience, love, endurance, persecutions, sufferings—what kinds of things happened to me in Antioch, Iconium and Lystra, the persecutions I endured. Yet the Lord rescued me from all of them" (3:10-11).

What that means, among other things, is that we significantly impact kids by creating vivid memories through which they watch, hear, see, or are touched by God at work. In short, we need to think of ourselves as not just program directors, but as memory makers.

What makes a memory memorable?

If you were to inventory the memories that shaped you, you'd probably find that one of the following factors made the occurrences memorable:

- **Surprise**. When we see something coming, it dulls our response.
- **Rarity**. We remember those moments when the extraordinary happened.
- **Uniqueness.** We remember facing a new challenge or experience.
- **Intensity.** Whether pleasant or painful, intense emotion seems to give a moment staying power.
- **Intimacy.** We are more apt to remember what we're personally involved in.
- **Risk.** There's a special exhilaration in attempting what we fear.
- **Ceremony.** Ceremonies are how we underline milestone moments with special recognition.

How memorable is your ministry?

Here's an informal self-test that can give you a feel about just how memorable your ministry is to your teenagers. In the chart below, write down the last five activities your youth group has done. Then for each of the activities, mark which memory-making elements were part of the event.

ACTIVITY	Surprise	Rarity	Uniqueness	Intensity	Intimacy	Risk	Ceremony
1.							
2.							
3.							
4.							
5.							

So is your ministry a hotbed of memories for your students? Or do you see now why your kids so easily forget youth group from one week to the next?

Making memories

As vital to your ministry as programs are, we hope this book helps you build more than programs—namely, memories. The 50 ideas here can help you usher your youth group (as individuals as well as a group) into wonderful experiences of God's grace and goodness.

Here are a few suggestions to help you become a memory maker:

• **Share the wealth.** No point in you having all the fun— particularly if you don't have a lot of time. So hand off selected ideas to volunteers, who probably have more time and energy for memory makers that require some preparation.

• **Adapt and experiment.** There's no such thing as a just-add-kids idea. Ideas don't work—youth workers work. Your job is to adapt the basic idea to the unique needs and personalities of the students in your group. Or use these ideas as springboards for thinking up your own memory makers from scratch.

• **Don't be discouraged if an idea doesn't work for you.** Each youth group—and each member in the group, of course—has a different personality. An idea that worked itself into the lore of one group may fizzle into ignominy for another group. So what? Relax and remember that God is in control.

• **Don't overdo a good thing.** The premise of *Memory Makers* can be dicey. After all, we're saying that contrived experiences can create the same sort of memories for a teenager or a youth group as unplanned, serendipitous happenings. So how do you engineer "spontaneous" moments to imitate truly unplanned times, like when the bus broke down and the group was stranded at a truck stop all night...or when you couldn't find where the youth choir was supposed to perform, so you all walked into a nearby rest home unannounced and asked if they'd like a concert...or when the tornado warning was sounded at your youth convention, so they herded all five thousand of you into the coliseum?

When you plan "spontaneity," it can look an awful lot like deception—which is not what we're advocating here. It's just that you may walk a fine line between surprise and trickery—though in our opinion these memory makers are good, clean, unmanipulative tricks. In any case, your attitude makes all the difference in the world.

• **Less is more.** Because some of these memory makers depend on surprise, you can't use them to effect more than once in five or six years or so. Unless, of course, you change jobs a lot.

• **Remember the Kodak moments.** Videotaping some of these memory makers—or even simply photographing them—will get you extra mileage from the events. Designate a student or volunteer as the official videographer (or photographer), and commission him or her to shoot lots of footage (or frames). The only thing that kids enjoy more than seeing themselves on screen and in photos is seeing themselves on a *big* screen and in *big* photos.

• **Have fun!** At least every now and then, take fun seriously.

UN-TESTIMONY SERVICE

≈ ≈ ≈ ≈ ≈ ≈ ≈

It's normal at the end of a retreat or camping week for students to verbalize publicly any spiritual decisions they've made. But what about those who *didn't* make a decision? Ask any of these kids (who are willing) to testify why they feel they cannot make a commitment yet. It's a perfect time for you to affirm sincere seekers in their search—and it promotes honest questions and candid ministry among group members.

MYSTERY HITCHHIKER

≈ ≈ ≈ ≈ ≈ ≈ ≈

What is your group's "compassion quotient"? If you're ready for a retreat on the subject, think about starting the retreat this way.

On the way to the retreat, drive your group by a staged car breakdown (the uglier and scuzzier the car, the better). Stop and offer to pick up the stranded driver—without letting anyone know that the person you're picking up is actually your retreat speaker. Arrange to have the speaker look as dilapidated as the car—dirty, smelly, unshaven, maybe acting a little strange. When you near your destination, drop the "stranger" off somewhere he can "get further help," then continue on to camp.

In the meantime, the speaker gets cleaned up and makes his way to camp (maybe with the help of one of your volunteers).

When the first session begins that night, introduce to your kids who the "stranger" actually is. Lay the weekend's foundation by discussing how they all responded with or without compassion to this stranger. Compassion will become more than a retreat theme to them.

BOWLING
TROPHIES
THAT BLESS

≈   ≈   ≈   ≈   ≈   ≈   ≈

The heart of a healthy ministry just may be the message behind a bowling trophy.

Healthy ministries are filled with appreciation and affirmation—and one easy, inexpensive way to express appreciation for your students is through personalized trophies. Don't spend big bucks on new ones—just buy old trophies from thrift stores (I've found dozens for a quarter each), then replace the dated plaque (1968 LADY BEES DIVISION FOUR CHAMPIONS) with a shiny new plaque that bears your own message (ANDY BRAZELTON: SERVANT OF THE MONTH). After spending a couple of dollars on the plaque, you'll have created an unusual treasure for the cost of lunch.

This is one memory maker that can become a regular award in your group. Heighten the anticipation of announcing the monthly or quarterly winner by keeping the trophy covered with a pillow case during the meeting, and then unveiling it as a surprise. You may be surprised how little it takes to make teenagers feel affirmed in their largely unaffirming world.

PREARRANGED DISASTER 1: RETREAT BUS BREAKDOWN

~ ~ ~ ~ ~ ~ ~

Why is it that kids usually talk more about the bus breaking down than about the retreat the bus was taking them to? Try staging a bus breakdown a mile from camp and have kids hike the last mile. (If your church bus is like most church vehicles, it may not even make it to the prearranged breakdown point.)

The best part comes as the kids near the camp and the "broken down" bus passes them with a huge sign on the back reading PIZZA HERE. After hiking a mile or two, they'll appreciate a good dinner—and a good laugh.

A variation of this bus-breakdown memory maker requires the group to stay on the retreat for another day. Secretly arrange it in advance with parents and the retreat center so the kids think they're getting an extra day.

SOUP-ER BOWL

~ ~ ~ ~ ~ ~ ~

A youth group we know organized 35 volunteers in their church to cook homemade chili. The students then went out on the street to invite homeless people in for a hot meal. The double surprise for these folks? They were being invited to a giant Super Bowl Party!

The youth group also invited members of the church to

drop by for a bowl of chili (for a small donation). The proceeds were donated to the local homeless shelter, and the homeless and the church congregation enjoyed each other's

company, the chili, and the Super Bowl.

PHOTOS GALORE

~ ~ ~ ~ ~ ~ ~

Adolescents love to look at themselves—in the mirror, in a photo, it makes no difference. You can use this trait of theirs to create a lasting memory in these students.

Take a photograph of you and the student, just your student, your small group, etc. Then have it printed on a coffee mug, T-shirt, enlarged into a calendar, placed in the face of a watch—the list of products on which you can put a photo is endless. Capture special events this way, too (camp, baptism, work projects), giving kids a lasting memento of a meaningful time in their lives.

SUNDAY SCHOOL INVASION

~ ~ ~ ~ ~ ~ ~

Imagine this: 15 minutes into your normal Sunday morning program, a uniformed police officer strides into your room. Can he talk to Aaron Smith, he asks. No, Aaron's not in trouble, he just wants to speak with him. The officer escorts Aaron to the parking lot—where you are waiting in your car, ready to take him to breakfast.

If you can't find a police officer, you could use a parent, an elder, or the pastor—anyone who can disrupt with authority and cause light embarrassment.

The point? You've invaded the normal Sunday schedule to spend some one-on-one time with a student. Sure, he'll miss the morning's teaching, but he would probably have forgotten it by Tuesday (and that's being generous). Besides, he'll have "teaching" he'll always remember.

RETREAT AT THE RITZ

~ ~ ~ ~ ~ ~ ~

Okay, it's not *the* Ritz, but it will feel like the Ritz compared to a lot of the retreat centers you've taken your group to. This idea works best if your group is on the small side, but you can make it work with a larger group, too.

Prep your students for the retreat the way you normally would. Dream up the name of some fictitious retreat center, and tell the kids to prepare for the usual camp weekend—sleeping bags, flashlights, insect repellent, that sort of thing.

Meanwhile, check around and find out if you can get some special weekend rates at a hotel within two or three hours of your church. Actually, many hotels' weekend rates are much more reasonable than their weekday rates—and you're probably going to put four kids in a room anyway. Off-season rates are better yet. Check around.

The fun comes when the bus is driving along the highway and you say, "You know what? I've changed my mind. Let's get some rooms at a hotel. What do you think?"

A Kentucky youth group we know got four rooms in Cincinnati at a three-star hotel—indoor pool, indoor volleyball, and indoor miniature golf. And because the hotel manager cut a deal on their food, it was actually cheaper than if they had gone to a camp.

But we know that veteran youth workers will probably miss those camp bunks.

AUDIO LETTER 1: SHOULD YOU CHOOSE TO ACCEPT THIS AFFIRMATION...

¿ ¿ ¿ ¿ ¿ ¿ ¿

The only thing more exciting to a teenager than getting a letter is getting a lumpy letter.

Imagine. You're 15 and your mom yells, "There's something in the mail for you." You run to the kitchen table, find the envelope with your name on it, tear into it, and find—an audio cassette? There's a Post-It note on it: "Wanted you to know how important you are." You stick the cassette in your tape deck, and hear a familiar voice: it's your favorite volunteer from church. She's talking to you—telling you how important you are to God and how much she likes spending time with you. She tells you that she knows God has an incredible future for you. She shares a Bible verse that's been on her mind today, then describes the Rottweiler about to jump out of the pickup in front of her.

"I'm terrible at writing letters," the tape concludes, "so I thought I'd speak one to you while I drove to work today. I just wanted you to know that I think about you and care for you."

You can buy a small recorder for $20. Keep it in your car for the times you feel like talking to this or that student.

BiRTHdAY VideO

Instead of spending a lot of money on birthday cards, grab an old video tape and make a video birthday card. Okay, the kid can't pin it to his bedroom wall, but a video "card" won't be thrown away with the other cards.

If you take some time and effort, the outcome is impressive. On a night when the teenager isn't home, sit down with her parents, pull out the photo album, and ask them to give you a visual tour of their teen's life through the album. You, of course, are armed with a vidcam, and you're getting all sorts of photos on video—including some embarrassing ones.

Next, interview some former Sunday school teachers, friends, extended family, and coaches—and ask them to tell stories about the birthday student.

Youth group is a perfect place to play this—but some students will get so jealous that they'll expect you to do this for *their* birthdays.

PREARRANGED DISASTER II: URBAN BUS BREAKDOWN

~ ~ ~ ~ ~ ~ ~

This time the bus breaks down in a bad part of town where you have (unbeknownst to the kids) already arranged to have the students housed for the night in a homeless shelter. Of course, make sure you secretly inform their parents of this—or the next prearranged disaster will be your termination as youth pastor.

CABIN SNEAK

~ ~ ~ ~ ~ ~ ~

In the early morning hours, the counselor of a camp cabin wakes up quietly and v-e-r-y carefully tip toes over to a chosen one of the sleeping bagged campers. Ever so quietly, the counselor awakens that camper: "Shhh. Don't say anything. I've got a plan, but we've got to be quiet. Get dressed. We're sneaking out of here."

At this point, there are a number of different options. One counselor and camper we heard "sneaked" down to the waterfront, where—with all the care of cat burglars—they untied a canoe, paddled to a restaurant across the lake, and had a delicious, hot breakfast.

Of course, the day before you've got to arrange for the canoe to be available. And if you're really brazen, tell the student afterward that your excursion is a secret only the two of you can share, "or else, you know, everybody will want to get into the act." That way, the next morning, you wake up early, and sneak out with *another* camper in your cabin.

It's a great chance for one-on-one time with a camper, and the camper goes home with a great memory. And one morning at least, you both get to eat *real* food.

YOUTHS ILLUSTRATED

～ ～ ～ ～ ～ ～ ～

Throw away your book of sermon illustrations. Your students can be a richer resource for illustrating your lesson points than any book. Your youths will feel not only known, but valued as well—and they'll remember it for a long time.

Okay, it sounds simple—but try it. Catch a student doing something right, hold her up as an example, and use the incident to support your point. For example, your text is Luke 11:5-8 and you want to illustrate persistence. You could say,

> *You probably heard that Julia got cut from the soccer team. I asked her how she felt about not making the team. Her honesty surprised me: she said she probably didn't deserve to make the team because she wasn't in good enough shape. She also said she was aiming at making the team next season—and she knows it will take specific, persistent training. Julia's not about to give up on her dream.*

You'll be surprised at how many illustrations walk through the youth room each week—and at the encouragement it is both for the group and for the individual.

GETTING ENGAGED WITH (NOT TO) YOUR STUDENTS

≈ ≈ ≈ ≈ ≈ ≈ ≈

This idea came from a youth worker who wanted his students to share a personal turning point in his life—his engagement. It's no secret that youth ministry is about sharing special moments in students' lives—but this idea sends the message that you care enough about them that you want them to share some of your personal moments as well.

A volunteer youth worker—call him Chad—made his engagement memorable for his future wife *and* his youth group. The day started with a picnic on the beach, where the girlfriend found a bottle from "a man on a deserted island." The bottle was planted by a student; it was also a student who was hidden behind the lifeguard tower, vidcam in hand, furtively catching the big event on tape. Students posing as tourists "happened" to gather and break into a medley of love songs. Other students reenacted the first time the couple met. Finally—also at the hands of the high schoolers—came a delicious catered meal, roses, and a card that popped the Big Question.

This husband and wife have a creative story to tell their grandchildren—and all the students involved in the event have a powerful memory of love, surprise, and making special moments memorable.

Try it with other special events, too: anniversaries, birthdays, graduations, Mother's Day, Father's Day, Valentine's Day, etc.

PLANNED MISCHIEF 1: TP BACKFIRE

An old prank with a twist. Plan with some of the kids to TP (a.k.a. toilet paper, wrap, etc.) the pastor's house. Since you value your relationship with the pastor, however—not to mention your job—arrange with him ahead of time to organize several members of the church board for a counterattack. At H hour, in the black of night, just as the kids are sneaking across the lawn, the pastor and his band of merry elders leap from the bushes with war whoops and water balloons flying.

GOOD SAM IN A CHEVY

Planning a Bible study about the parable of the Good Samaritan? A half hour before the study, and a block or two away from the church—that is, right along the route your students take to church—plant a car breakdown with the driver out trying to flag down cars for a ride to a service station, for help with a flat tire, etc. The driver should be of a different ethnic or racial background from the majority of your students (and probably a woman, perhaps with small children, so there's no excuse that passers-by are intimidated about picking up a menacing stranger).

As you begin the Bible study, the woman walks in—and you'll have no trouble getting students to discuss how easy it is to pass by people in need.

PHONE MEMORY 1: SURPRISE SPEAKER-PHONE INCIDENT

~ ~ ~ ~ ~ ~ ~

David Letterman has made an art form out of impromptu phone calls. It's actually easy enough for a youth group to pull off—and it makes for some interesting memories. All it requires is a basic speaker phone and enough phone cable to connect your phone to the nearest jack. No phone jacks where you meet? Then use a cellular phone, and hook a speaker up to the receiving end. Then start making memorable calls:

• Call group members who aren't at youth group that night.

• Take the speaker phone along on a retreat; each night let a student call home to her parents.

• Find a mom or dad with a birthday that night, and have the entire youth group sing "Happy Birthday."

• Sing "Happy Birthday" to your pastor (on his birthday).

• Call a group member who is in the hospital.

• Call the youth pastor's parents, and interview them

about the youth pastor's teenage years.

• Call a youth group graduate who's away at college.

Getting Clean

~ ~ ~ ~ ~ ~ ~

Following the Lord's example in John 13, have students wash each other's feet. In the center of a circle of students (10 or less), provide two or three small basins of water and a few towels. Appropriate background music or group singing helps establish the tone of the ceremony—quiet, reflective, prayerful. One at a time, students wash the feet of another person.

You can structure the time more or less with variations like these: participants can wash the feet of a

person they have come to know better, a person from whom they've felt genuine love, a person they really admire, a person they'd like to know better.

This act of humility gives the youths a vivid reminder that we are called to be servants. Selflessness is a rare thing in today's society; if it is visually etched in their minds, it will be remembered.

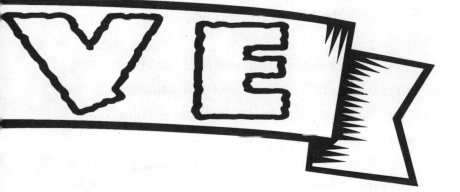

AFFIRMATION CIRCLE

Most students we meet are dying for encouragement—especially from peers. Help fill this need with life-changing encouragement by setting aside some time during the last night of camp for your students to affirm character qualities in one another.

If possible, organize kids in groups of a dozen or less. Supply each individual with a pencil and as many 3 x 5 cards as there are members in the small group. Then ask them to write one, two, or three qualities (depending on available time and size of group) they appreciate about each person in their small group (one person's traits per card).

Then gather everyone into one circle and choose one person to be encouraged; members of his small group read what they've written about him, then pass to him "his" cards as a reminder of the affirming words. Do this with everyone. You'll be surprised how genuine encouragement from peers can affect the entire youth group.

AUDIO LETTER II: MORNING DRIVE SURPRISE

∿ ∿ ∿ ∿ ∿ ∿ ∿

Get the cooperation of a student's parent or friend to stash the cassette you record—a greeting, brief encouragement, a devotional thought, or just a unique greeting—in the tape deck of the car the student takes to school. Make sure you or your accomplice cues up the tape, turns the deck on, and turns up the volume so that the tape begins playing as soon as the car is turned on—or, if it's not the teenager's own car, as soon as he's in the car he takes to school.

So on a dreary Monday morning the engine cranks up, and like magic the student hears your voice: "Hey, Jenny, just wanted to say hi—and to let you know how much I appreciated you sharing last week at youth group..."

This is also a great memory maker for kids to create for their parents—particularly on Mother's or Father's Day.

"GOOD MORNING RALPHY!"

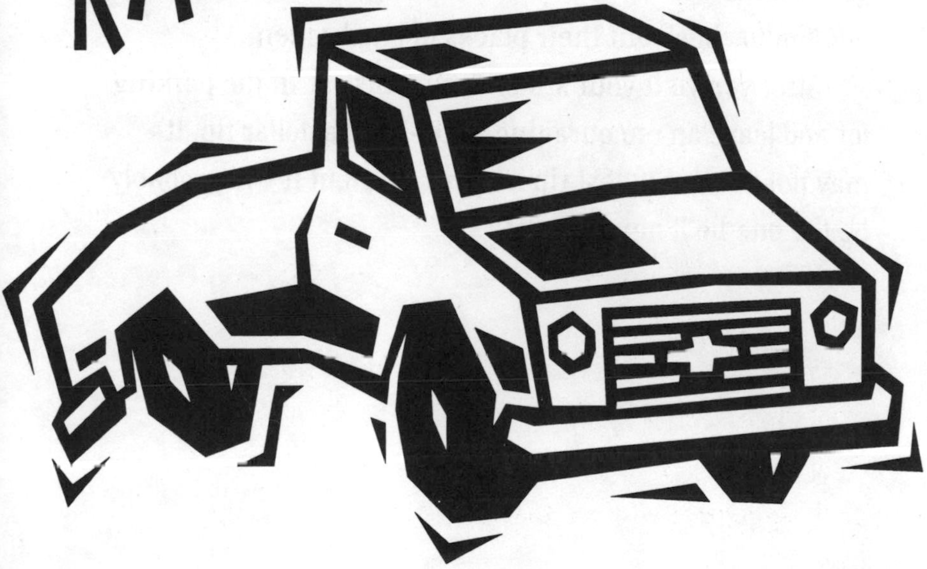

FAST-FOOD
TIPS

～ ～ ～ ～ ～ ～ ～

The kind of McJobs your students probably hold are often thankless, minimum-wage affairs. So it's always fun for them to get a visit, during working hours, from their youth pastor or volunteer youth worker. If worktime visits are appropriate—that is, if the student employees don't get in trouble for it—they'll be thrilled that you cared enough to check out their places of employment.

After you visit your student, find his car in the parking lot and leave an encouraging note—and a dollar tip. It may not be the biggest tip he ever gets, but it will probably be the one he'll never forget.

THIS PRESENT DARKNESS ALL-NIGHTER

〜 〜 〜 〜 〜 〜 〜

Need some good lock-in material? Best-selling Christian novelist Frank Peretti provides an intriguing story of spiritual warfare in *This Present Darkness*. It comes alive with graphic descriptions of demons and angels and how they protect and destroy people within a town. It has all the enticing elements of a murder mystery, is a vivid portrayal of spiritual warfare, and really gets you thinking about prayer and Christians' roles in their community.

So buy the audio tape version of the novel before your next all-nighter, and schedule three one-hour sessions to listen to the book. Switch off the lights, light some candles—and be prepared to discuss the spiritual battle that Scripture warns us about. Your students won't easily forget this night.

TAKE IT TO THE CROSS

~ ~ ~ ~ ~ ~ ~

The forgiveness that Jesus gives can be difficult to comprehend. So help kids visualize it during a camp or special program by having students anonymously write down a sin or sins they are currently struggling with. After your talk about forgiveness, bring to the front a rough wooden cross pieced together before the meeting; at its foot place a hammer and a box of nails (sixpenny nails do fine). Invite students to come forward and nail their written confessions to the cross. It's a visual (and possibly emotionally intense) way for kids to understand Christ's forgiveness—and the power he has to give them a brand-new start.

ON THE GO

A large U-Haul or Ryder truck (or any utility truck) can be the site of a truly moving memory. Rent one and fill it with your youth room's furniture (or furniture very like that in your youth room)—couches, bean bag chairs, photographs, posters, boombox, everything. Decorate the inside of the truck so it resembles as closely as possible your youth room or the home in which you normally meet.

Add a supply of food, then you're ready to take your traveling meeting room on the road. Drive to the site where you usually hold the meeting, and invite the kids into the truck instead. Or (if state laws permit it) pick up kids at their homes or at church, then truck them all somewhere else for the meeting. Or get a volunteer to drive, and you conduct the meeting during the drive. (Make sure you have proper ventilation in the truck, or you'll need a book on creating memorable funerals.)

SHOTGUN DISCIPLESHIP

∾ ∾ ∾ ∾ ∾ ∾ ∾

Whether you've been in youth ministry 10 months or 10 years, you know the adolescent claim well (usually shouted, and accompanied by racing and jostling): "*Shotgun!*" Students want to feel important, grown-up, and valued, and many feel this way when they ride in the front.

So take advantage of your personal errand running by asking a student to join you. Some of the best conversations we've had with students came while picking up groceries or running down to the hardware store. Even without an agenda, it's still a time of incognito discipleship.

The day Carl and I built a doghouse, we drove around the city picking up lumber and shingles—and talked about everything. The doghouse was pretty much a loss—it lasted one winter. But judging from conversations with Carl since then, memories of that day have lasted a long time for Carl.

Whether kids ride shotgun or work at your house,

these no-agenda times are a genuine way for students to *see* the Jesus they hear about on Sundays lived out in a Monday-through-Saturday way.

THIS IS YOUR DAY

    Choose a special student in your group who's either in need of a huge dose of encouragement, or one you want to reward for her advancement within your discipleship process. Then dedicate your next program to this teenager. Hang banners proclaiming her name around the room. Show baby pictures. Show video interviews of teachers, friends, and parents on special qualities they've observed in her. Get the entire youth group involved by asking them trivia questions about her life. Then teach on a distinctive characteristic she embodies—a trait that can apply to the whole group.

    The time you spend in preparation is a small investment in a young person's life, with returns you may never fully realize.

PLANNED MISCHIEF 11: DITCHING SUNDAY SCHOOL

~ ~ ~ ~ ~ ~ ~

You just aren't normal if you haven't wanted, at least once in your life, to ditch Sunday school. Don't flatter yourself—your students are no exceptions.

So just do it! Especially if you have a small group, it's not that hard to slide out the classroom door, saunter down the hallway, slip out of the building, and slink down the street to the corner coffee shop with a few of your buds.

If your group is too large to inconspicuously leave the church, arrange for one of your teachers to sneak out with his small group.

And here's where the fun begins: when you get to the coffee shop, who do you find sipping a mug of decaf but the pastor. Sure it's planned, but you feign embarrassment anyway and ask him if he'll join you at a table.

So begins your group's private audience with the pastor—and what could be the most memorable Sunday school your group has ever had. And there's a bonus: since most of the students won't have money, the pastor can pay the tab. He'll only be experiencing what you go through every week.

TOUR
OF YOUR LIFE

～ ～ ～ ～ ～ ～ ～

This is a day-long teaching event that hits the road. It begins with a morning tour of the maternity ward of a hospital, where guided discussion explores the dreams and fears your teenagers' parents might have had for them the day they were born. Then on through the various stages of life—a stop at an elementary school, a park's playground (complete with swing and jungle gym), the junior high and high school, a college, two or three local work places (blue collar, white collar, self-employed, etc.), a retirement home. Your final stop is a funeral home.

At each stop encourage the kids to record their thoughts in a journal or share them in group discussion. Each location—that is, each stage of life—raises questions and issues that are offered up for reflection. Use the small chapel that the funeral home will probably have to conduct your choice of worship experience or service of commitment.

ReTReAT AT THe TOP OF THe WORLD

‹› ‹› ‹› ‹› ‹› ‹› ‹›

It requires some phone work, but this is a lock-in your kids will never forget—especially if snow skiing is in your plans.

Most larger ski resorts have some sort of accommodations in or near the lift house at the top of the slope—as meager as a rustic lodge, as sumptuous as a restaurant. Either variety will do as long as it has rest rooms of some sort.

Contact the resort and ask if you can book that top-of-the-slope facility for an all-nighter—at the "top of the world."

One youth worker we know organized a lock-in on New Year's Eve in the lodge atop a ski resort in the Poconos. He arranged with the resort management to have his kids ride back up the mountain after the lifts closed for the day. The resort allowed him and his group to spend the night on top of the mountain, where they all sleeping-bagged it in the dining hall. (A volunteer drove the bags and other supplies up the service road to the top of the mountain.)

And with any luck and some extra bucks, you might persuade the resort to cater dinner for your group. At least you can probably grill your own burgers and hot dogs outside.

Imagine your group enjoying dinner together at the top of the slope, meeting together around the stone hearth of a fireplace, and then topping it all off with some videos, games, and a sunrise service like they've never seen.

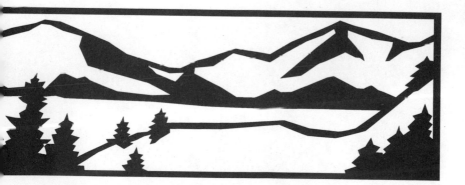

PREARRANGED DISASTER III: POWER OUTAGE

~ ~ ~ ~ ~ ~ ~

Privately plan a power outage on the last night of camp. Complete darkness limits your options of activities, but increases your potential for conversation and memories. Total-darkness conditions make for fun hours around the campfire, everyone in sleeping bags in the kerosene-lamp-lit dining hall or chapel—or wonderfully suspenseful episodes of Capture the Flag. (This idea works best when the youth staff is under 30 years old.)

WORLD SHOE RELIEF

~ ~ ~ ~ ~ ~ ~

Serious runners put only a few hundred miles on their shoes before replacing them, usually because the sole is "packed"—that is, it's become hard, and a packed sole can cause shin splints and knee injuries to a serious runner. But otherwise the shoe is still in excellent condition.

And people in desperate need of shoes don't care if the soles are packed.

Ask your students to begin asking around at athletic-equipment stores for these shoes. With a few fliers left on the counters at such stores, you'll find runners happy to give these shoes away.

Once your students have gathered a box or two of shoes, take them to a homeless shelter and distribute them. This is an easy way to get some of your students involved in a missions project that doesn't include crossing the border.

LeTTeR FROM GOD

~ ~ ~ ~

It's a stretch for many kids to believe that God's Word is relevant. What could it possibly say to them and their problems and passions? Try writing a letter to a student—a letter composed by stringing a few Bible verses together, paraphrased just enough to make it flow. (Just be careful you don't contort the meaning of the verses by the context you give them.*) If you choose your selections well from Scripture, you can produce a letter with genuine meaning and value to the student.

(Early in my ministry someone anonymously sent me a letter like this. You can't imagine what it meant to me. I taped it into the front of my planning calendar, and I've carried it with me ever since.)

Dear Brian,

I have created you. I've called you by name. You are precious in my sight, and I rejoice over you with joy. In fact, I called you into fellowship with my son, Jesus.

I taught you how to walk in my ways, though you may not have realized it. So seek me day by day, and delight to know my ways. Press on to know me, and I will respond to you as surely as the coming of the dawn or the rain of early spring. Come and behold my beauty, Brian. Pour out your heart to me like water, and know the refreshment that comes from my presence.

Love always,
Your heavenly Father
(Brian—the text of this letter is directly from God's Word. Here's where you can find the verses, in the order they appeared above: Isaiah 43:1; Isaiah 43:4; Zephaniah 3:17; 1 Corinthians 1:9; Hosea 11:3; Isaiah 58:2; Hosea 6:3; Psalm 27:4; Lamentations 2:19; Acts 3:19)

---

* It's horrifically easy, of course, to use this idea to bludgeon a kid's ego, warp his perception of God, or ravage accepted principles of biblical interpretation—all by ignoring the context of the verses. Case in point:

Dear Bearl,
Because of you I will weep and wail; I will go about barefoot and naked. I will howl like a jackal and moan like an owl.
Seventy kings with their thumbs and big toes cut off have picked up scraps under my table. On the other hand, you may eat any animal that has a split hoof divided in two and that chews the cud. Of all the creatures living in the water, you may eat any that has fins and scales.
Then take a spike and push it through his ear lobe into the door, and he will become your servant for life.
Designate a place outside the camp where you can go to relieve yourself. Then you will know the refreshment that comes from my presence.
(Scripture references, in order: Micah 1:8; Judges 1:7; Deuteronomy 14:6; Deuteronomy 14:9; Deuteronomy 15:17; Deuteronomy 23:12; Acts 3:19)

RAISE AN EBENEZER

You probably recognize that phrase, "Here I raise mine Ebenezer" from "Come Thou Fount of Every Blessing." So what (or who) exactly is an Ebenezer, and how do you raise it?

First of all, Ebenezer means *stone of help*—specifically, it was a stone that the prophet Samuel set up to commemorate a military victory over the Philistines (1 Samuel 7:10-13). "Thus far has the Lord helped us," he said as he set up the stone monument.

So the next time you close out a retreat or camp, tell your students to walk the grounds and find a rock that indicates what God has done in them during the retreat. They should bring their rocks back home to the youth room; there you can lead your students in an "Ebenezer service" by asking them to pile up all their rocks: a modern-day Ebenezer! Build your commemorative pile in the church lobby, in a Sunday school classroom, in the youth room itself, outside where it can be seen regularly—anywhere it can remind your kids of God's

goodness and their decisions during that retreat or
camp.

ONE SWEET LETTER

~ ~ ~ ~ ~ ~ ~

On your way home, stop by a convenience store and buy a handful of candy bars—but not just any candy bar. Select those whose names you can incorporate in an affirming letter to a student. You know, "Hey, BIG HUNK— there's no room for any SNICKERS when I say that I'd have to go to MARS to find someone to do as good a job in last Sunday's youth service as you did..."

Write the letter on a big sheet of card stock, then tape or glue on the candy bars themselves in place of the words they stand for.

PLANNED MISCHIEF III: CABIN RAID BACKFIRE

~ ~ ~ ~ ~ ~ ~

It's just a 2 a.m. water balloon raid against another cabin. Or so you'll let on to *your* cabin. What your campers don't know is that you've made secret arrangements with the counselor of the other cabin.

So your cabin's students slink out under cover of darkness, expecting to douse slumbering, unsuspecting victims. Meanwhile, the "victims" have hidden themselves outside of and around their cabin. Just about the time the attackers enter the cabin—and discover that no one's home—out of their hiding places charge the others with a rebel yell. It's a massacre that'll be remembered for a long time.

FUTURE FRESHMAN

∾ ∾ ∾ ∾ ∾ ∾ ∾

The freshman year can be a traumatic transition for kids. Maybe you can make it a bit easier with a personal letter to one of your incoming freshmen (or some, or all). Encourage them with what God can do in them during their high school years. Warn them of the pressures they'll likely face. Give them something to strive for. Maybe something like this:

Dear Elissa,

Welcome to your freshman year! It's been great getting to know you this summer, and I'm thrilled about you being part of the senior high youth group.

You're in for a real adventure during the next four years. And I'm confident, Elissa, that you've got what it takes to survive high school, and even thrive there, too.

When I talk about surviving high school, I'm not talking about avoiding getting stuffed in the trash can by a senior. I mean spiritual survival. I've watched a lot of students get overwhelmed by pressures and temptations, and finally graduate not only from high school but from their faith as well. It's not that there aren't enough Bible studies and choir tours and mission trips for them—it's usually that they simply make wrong choices.

During the next four years you'll see and hear a lot. With any luck—and some wise choices on your part—you'll experience a lot of fun, positive moments in the halls and classrooms and labs and locker rooms. But you'll inevitably see and hear a lot of junk, too—more parties, sexual predicaments, alcohol and drug abuse, and fights than you've been exposed to yet. They'll seem strange at first—but the more you're exposed to them, the more they appear natural, cool, even glamorous. And finally legitimate.

So it can be tough to be known as a Christian on the Montrose H.S. campus. If you do let your faith be known, some kids will admire you, and some will ignore you. Yet if you stand firm and do not compromise your faith during your freshman year, you'll earn the respect of many of your peers. They'll gradually understand that you're not just a religious person, but that you have an authentic faith that wears well in the pressure cooker of high school. Your friends, meanwhile, will respect and appreciate you for your integrity, for standing firm.

You're a popular girl, Elissa, and many people will look to you to see how you handle yourself during difficult situations—though you probably won't be aware of being watched. Nevertheless, they'll watch how you talk, how you treat others, how you perform under pressure. Like it or not, Christians are watched.

I believe in you, Elissa. And I believe that you have what it takes to survive high school and even thrive there as a growing Christian. I can hardly wait to see how the hands of your kind and gracious God shape and mold you over the next four years. I want you to know that I'm here for you as a friend and a sister. I look forward to your high school graduation, when you can look back on four years that were sometimes rough, sometimes fun—but they will have been four years of doing your best to be an example of a Christian.

I care about you!
Sue

COMPLETE THE SENTENCE

∿ ∿ ∿ ∿ ∿ ∿ ∿

Think up some affirming greetings, write 'em down, then photocopy them onto card stock—at least, the *beginnings* of some greetings. Sentence starters like these:

- Today I was thinking about you, and—
- I'm glad you're in our youth group because—
- I don't believe what everybody says about you because—

Pass them out formally or casually to your students, encouraging them to finish the sentences and then mail

 the postcards to a friend. Fill out and mail some yourself to let absent kids know you were thinking of them.

DOUBLE PHOTOS, DOUBLE BLESSINGS

~ ~ ~ ~ ~ ~ ~

And now for a word from the Sheesh After All These Years I've Been Making Photo Collages For The Youth Room You Would've Thought I'd Think Of This Idea department: for just a few pennies more, you can get a second set of prints of your youth group photos. Use these "seconds"  as opportunities to write a letter now and then to kids— and enclose photographic "trophies" with your letters. You know how students love to get mail—and how they love seeing themselves in pictures. Just another visual reminder for a student that he or she is important to you.

PERFORM-A-PROM

If you have reason to schedule an alternative to the high school's Christmas dance or year-end prom, have fun with it! Serve your students dinner in an unusual place—on top of the (flat) church roof, in an empty pool or an empty lot. Borrow the nicest car a church member has to offer and chauffeur the kids. Find some red carpet to unroll for them as they enter and exit the car. Put a camera or a vidcam in the hands of an accomplice, and get the evening on film or tape.

Conclude your dinner and dance with dinner aboard a flatbed or (clean) dump truck—or even a fire truck, if you can swing it.

Pretend your students are royalty—then let your imagination go crazy to give them a night they'll never forget.

PREARRANGED DISASTER IV: LOST BUS

The story behind this memory maker? Well, we *really* got lost once. And it became part of the youth group's lore.

So you leave church one Friday night after dark, bound for a retreat center. The bus driver then takes a route calculated to get the group "hopelessly lost" out in the country somewhere.

The hour grows later, and the group becomes starkly aware of the futility of the situation. With a hint of frustration in your voice, suggest to the driver—but loud enough to be heard by the front third of the bus—that you all find some campground or rest area where the bus load of kids can spend the night. (You've arranged this in advance, of course. It could be a picnic area that allows overnight parking, or a campground whose manager will play along to be grumpy and reluctant but finally willing to let you park the bus overnight. And you stashed—secretly, or under a pretense—a cooler of ice, drinking water and drinks, snack food, flashlights, candles or lanterns, toilet paper, and the like.)

In any case, you want the kids marooned on the bus all night—telling stories, playing games, singing, praying, harassing the driver who got them "lost."

Early Saturday morning, one of your volunteers flags down a passing motorist who happens to know where the retreat center is and agrees to lead you there. What the kids don't know is that the motorist is actually another of your contacts, who leads the bus to yet *another* roadside picnic area—but here parents have prepared a huge, hot breakfast for everyone.

After breakfast it's on to the retreat center for hot showers and the remainder of the weekend. Incidentally, this is one way to start students thinking about your retreat theme, especially if it's about being lost, finding the way, light for a dark road, etc.

ADJECTIVE OVERLOAD

Students thrive on encouragement—even simple encouragement like this:

Write the student's name in the middle of a sheet of paper. Then surround the name with all sorts of descriptive words that fit the student. Add to the impact of this gift letter by having someone with computer or graphic skills lay out the words for a more formal presentation. For a *really* formal presentation, frame it.

notices
little things

eager
to help

good friend

Jonathan

makes you
laugh

kind

compassionate

loyal

great smile

CUSTOMIZED POSTERS

∾　∾　∾　∾　∾　∾　∾

You've seen the posters typically sold in Christian bookstores—Bible verses or otherwise inspirational phrases printed over landscapes, action shots of athletes, footprints on a beach, cuddly animals. Ready for a change? Your own youth group poster!

Film developers—the chains as well as the labs that professionals use—can take any slide or print of yours, enlarge it, lay over it any text you want, and print it on paper stock.

• Extend the memories of summer camp with a group-designed poster of the verse, "Being confident of this, that he who began a good work in you will carry it on to completion until the day of Christ Jesus" (Phil. 1:6), laid over a favorite camp photo.

• To remember a work project: "Don't let anyone look down on you because you are young, but set an example for the believers in speech, in life, in love, in faith and in purity" (1 Tim. 4:12).

• To commemorate a student's participation in your

annual Mud Bowl fundraiser: "You are clean, though not every one of you" (John 13:10b).

Of course, after these posters hang in the youth room for a month or two, take them down and give them as gifts (or sell them as fundraisers) to kids or parents.

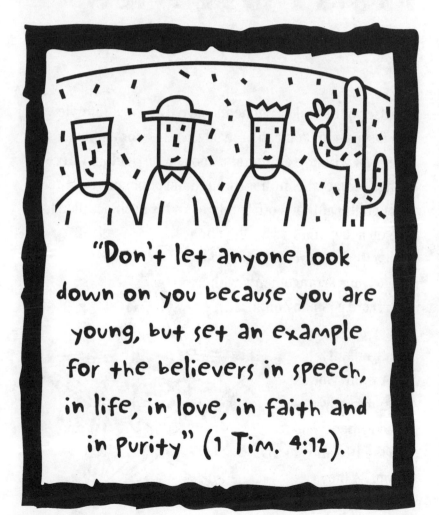

"Don't let anyone look down on you because you are young, but set an example for the believers in speech, in life, in love, in faith and in purity" (1 Tim. 4:12).

PHONE MEMORY 11: SPEAKER-PHONE ARTIST INTERVIEW

∾ ∾ ∾ ∾ ∾ ∾ ∾

Use your speaker phone to add a live-voice interview to a discussion. You can probably arrange for a phone interview with the author of a book or curriculum you're using (contact the author through the publisher or through the author's office address). It's even possible to line up a few minutes on the phone with a Christian recording artist (make your arrangements with the record company or artist's personal management).

A youth worker we know showed a video by Geoff Moore and the Distance to his group. As they discussed the video, he said, "I thought you might be interested in talking with the guy who wrote that song." And there on the phone was Geoff Moore, with whom the kids were able to talk about the lyrics, about the video, about Geoff's message.

Sure, this takes some work—and not all artists are as cooperative as Geoff Moore—but the result of the memory is worth a try.

Good Morning, America

~ ~ ~ ~ ~ ~ ~

A tried-and-true memory maker is still the good ol' wake-up call. Just let the parents in on what you'll do, and take a vidcam in tow. Here are some ideas that have worked for us:

• Go to your student's home in a gorilla costume, so she'll think she's being awakened by King Kong.

- Operate a leaf blower outside the student's window—or in his room.
- Take with you a few students, and serve the wakee a McDonald's breakfast in bed.
- Wake her up by singing Christmas carols.
- Is it his birthday? Wake him up with a rousing 6 a.m. rendition of "Happy Birthday"—and then out to the kitchen for a birthday (pan)cake breakfast.

LOVE THAT LAUNDRY

〜 〜 〜 〜 〜 〜 〜

This memory maker isn't as much for your students as for their moms—or whoever does the family laundry.

Lead a letter-writing campaign—letters by the teenagers, to their moms, and deposited in their pants pockets. When Mom goes through all the pockets before she tosses the pants into the washing machine, she'll find a letter of appreciation—to her!

At a youth group meeting, give each of your students five or ten index cards on which they write brief thank-you notes to their moms. Nothing fancy—just a simple thank-you for doing so much of the dirty work around the old homestead: "Dear Mom—Thanks for washing these grubby jeans one more time. I know I don't often thank you for all the stuff you do around here, but I really appreciate it. You're great, Mom!"

On an appointed date, the students begin stuffing these thank-you notes, one at a time, into their pants pockets just before they throw them into the dirty-clothes hamper. And sometime that week a dozen or so moms will stand over their teenagers' mounds of dirty underwear and socks, gratitude in their hearts—and just maybe tears in their eyes.

YOUTH GROUP MEMORY CHEST

~ ~ ~ ~ ~ ~ ~

You call it a box of memories. Your spouse calls it junk. "Why are you saving this *bowling pin*, for crying out loud?" you're asked. At which point you get a bit defensive, and so launch into a story about the profound emotional significance the bowling pin has for you. If your house caught fire, you'd grab your family, your Day-Timer, and that box.

Pragmatic spouses aside, why not lead your group in stockpiling a chest of memories? Plop down an empty box some night in front of your teenagers, and explain how you all will retain memories from your upcoming events: after each of your events, your students should decide on what item is the best memory holder for that event. Anything can work—a shattered Ping-Pong paddle from your game night, a broken ski-boot binding from the snow trip, a brick from the work project, a broken nose from the discipline problem, a pizza crust from the overnighter (you'd better shellac it so it doesn't grow mold).

Make your New Year's Eve party a time for going

through the memory chest and talking through the year's events, stories, and commitments. Then divvy up the treasures among the graduating seniors the following June as farewell gifts.

THIRD TIMOTHY

〜 〜 〜 〜 〜 〜 〜

You could say that St. Paul was a big brother of sorts to the young pastor Timothy, who probably read the two letters from his apostolic mentor with respect and admiration for the solid counsel the older Christian gave him.

This same Paul-Timothy relationship often happens within a youth group—though it's not always obvious because younger students seldom admit that they admire an older peer. Yet we know how effective peer ministry is, how students will listen to each other before they listen to adults.

Take advantage of this tendency by asking some of your graduating students to write a letter to their youth group. Maybe start them off this way: "If you could say anything you wanted to the group, what would it be?" Because of your group's size, you might want each senior to write a letter to a particular grade or class.

At whatever time you graduate out your seniors, have them read their farewell letters aloud to the group. Some letters may be worthy of lamination, framing, and hanging in the youth room.

We the seniors bid you farewell and remind you of the way our

PLANNED MISCHIEF IV: A WELCOME GLUT OF JUNK MAIL

~ ~ ~ ~ ~ ~ ~

We can't remember a youth group grad who, especially during her freshman year, didn't crave mail. Now this memory maker sound trivial, we know—but it works! Kids love even *this* kind of mail.

What kind of mail, you ask. You know those card decks you get in the mail—an inch-thick, shrink-wrapped stack of postcard-sized advertisements for various products? If you don't find them in your mailbox, they fall out of new magazines you flip through. These cards are self-addressed and postage-paid for convenient, speedy return.

Here's what to do: deluge your freshman friend with mail by filling out these free cards with the student's new college address. The result: she'll get junk mail for months to come! (Actually, to freshmen we know, there's hardly such a thing as junk mail.)

You may want to send her a personal note explaining that you've made some arrangements for her to get some mystery mail—and that every time she gets a strange something-or-other in the mail, it should serve as a reminder of your love for her. So when sample copies of *Vegetarian Digest*, *Boy's Life*, *Mutual Funds Report*, and *Mechanics Illustrated* arrive in her mailbox, they just may become fun remembrances of a youth director back home thinking of her.

FiNALS WEEK SURVIVAL KiT

∾ ∾ ∾ ∾ ∾ ∾ ∾

To a high schooler, the end of a semester is more grueling than the Spanish Inquisition: in addition to the regular homework are tons of late assignments to turn in, papers and projects are due, kids are cramming for finals. "Too much homework," they'll lament when you ask them if they're coming to youth group that week.

Make this hectic time a bit more bearable by delivering to each student's home a Finals Week Survival Kit: studying essentials like candy bars, a six-pack of soda, maybe some encouraging Scriptures, two or three colors of highlighter felt pens, and travel-size mouthwash for the all-nighters. (My rule of thumb: if it tastes good and is high in sugar, put it in the kit. And if your kids can take a mild ribbing, include a photocopy of your high school diploma with a note on it that you don't have to take any more finals and can watch TV until midnight with impunity.)

PRE-CAMP PARENT LETTER

A week or so before your church's teens go to summer camp, suggest to their parents that they write their kids a letter—which the teenagers read after they get to camp.

The letters should include words from parent to kid that express affirmation, appreciation, encouragement... how the parent views the teenager's Christian commitment...the significance of that child in his or her family...how much the kid will be missed.

Some parents will need some pointers—and perhaps even an outline—to get them started. So go ahead and give them examples of letters you've written, of affirming letters written to you (that you want to share this way as examples)—whatever facilitation or encouragement they need to write their kids. The bottom line is for parents to put their love into words.

At camp give the students their letters—and give them a half hour or so of private, quiet time afterwards. For many students, the letters may be a rare moment of parental affirmation.

HAVE SOME
FIELD-TESTED
MEMORY MAKERS
OF YOUR OWN?

Want to contribute them to the next *Memory Makers*? You'll get your name in the book, a few bucks in your pocket, and the satisfaction of passing along an effective memory maker to thousands of youth workers like you. Send your ideas to Memory Makers, 21612 Plano Trabuco Q-30, Trabuco Canyon, CA 92679.

YOUTH SPECIALTIES TITLES

Professional Resources

Developing Spiritual Growth in Junior High Students
Developing Student Leaders
Equipped to Serve: Volunteer Youth Worker Training Course
Help! I'm a Sunday School Teacher!
Help! I'm a Volunteer Youth Worker!
How to Expand Your Youth Ministry
How to Recruit and Train Volunteer Youth Workers
The Ministry of Nurture
One Kid at a Time
Peer Counseling in Youth Groups
Advanced Peer Counseling in Youth Groups

Discussion Starter Resources

Get 'Em Talking
4th-6th Grade TalkSheets
High School TalkSheets
Junior High TalkSheets
High School TalkSheets: Psalms and Proverbs
Junior High TalkSheets: Psalms and Proverbs
More High School TalkSheets
More Junior High TalkSheets
Parent Ministry TalkSheets
What If...? Provocative Questions to Get Teenagers Talking, Thinking, Doing
Would You Rather...? 465 Questions to Get Kids Talking

Ideas Library

Combos: 1-4, 5-8, 9-12, 13-16, 17-20, 21-24, 25-28, 29-32, 33-36, 37-40, 41-44, 45-48, 49-52
Singles: 53, 54, 55
Ideas Index

Youth Ministry Programming

Compassionate Kids: Practical Ways to Involve Kids in Mission and Service
Creative Bible Lessons in John: Encounters with Jesus
Creative Bible Lessons on the Life of Christ
Creative Programming Ideas for Junior High Ministry
Creative Socials and Special Events
Dramatic Pauses
Facing Your Future
Great Fundraising Ideas for Youth Groups
Great Retreats for Youth Groups
Greatest Skits on Earth
Greatest Skits on Earth, Vol. 2
Hot Illustrations for Youth Talks
More Hot Illustrations for Youth Talks
Hot Talks
Incredible Questionnaires for Youth Ministry
Junior High Game Nights
More Junior High Game Nights
Play It! Great Games for Groups
Play It Again! More Great Games for Groups
Road Trip
Super Sketches for Youth Ministry
Teaching the Bible Creatively
Up Close and Personal: How to Build Community in Your Youth Group

(continued on next page)

Clip Art

ArtSource Vol. 1—Fantastic
    Activities
ArtSource Vol. 2—Borders,
    Symbols, Holidays, and
    Attention Getters
ArtSource Vol. 3—Sports
ArtSource Vol. 4—Phrases and
    Verses
ArtSource Vol. 5—Amazing
    Oddities and Appalling Images
ArtSource Vol. 6—Spiritual Topics
ArtSource Vol. 7—Variety Pack

Videos

Edge TV
God Views
The Heart of Youth Ministry: A
    Morning with Mike Yaconelli
Next Time I Fall in Love Video
    Curriculum
Promo Spots for Junior High Game
    Nights
Understanding Your Teenager
    Video Curriculum

Student Books

Grow For It Journal
Grow For It Journal through the
    Scriptures
Next Time I Fall in Love
Wild Truth Journal for Junior
    Highers
101 Things to Do during a Dull
    Sermon